RECORD-B... WEATHER

by Thea Feldman

Glenview, Illinois
Boston, Massachusetts
Chandler, Arizona
Upper Saddle River, New Jersey

Picture Credits
Every effort has been made to secure permission and provide appropriate credit for photographic material.
The publisher deeply regrets any omission and pledges to correct errors called to its attention in subsequent editions.

Unless otherwise acknowledged, all photographs are the copyright © of Dorling Kindersley, a division of Pearson.

Photo locators denoted as follows: Top (T), Center (C), Bottom (B), Left (L), Right (R), Background (Bkgd).

Opener: (Bkgd) James Leynse/Corbis; 1 (C) ©DK Images; 2 Digital Vision; 4 (B) Tui De Roy/Minden Pictures; 7 James Leynse/Corbis; 9 (B) Jim Reed/Corbis; 10 (B) Steve Starr/Corbis; 13 Mike Berger and Jim Reed/Photo Researchers, Inc.; 14 (T) Tui De Roy/Minden Pictures, (B) James Leynse/Corbis, (B) Mike Berger and Jim Reed/Photo Researchers, Inc.

FP4 (B) Tui De Roy/Minden Pictures; FP6 (B) ©DK Images.

ISBN-13: 978-0-328-65770-4
ISBN-10: 0-328-65770-0

4 5 6 7 8 9 10 V0FL 14 13 12

What You Already Know

Weather is what's happening with the air in the atmosphere. Atmosphere is the name given to the blanket of air that surrounds Earth and separates it from outer space. It has different layers, and different properties at each layer.

Meteorologists study the weather, including temperature and wind. Changes in air pressure generally lead to changes in weather. Low-pressure air usually brings clouds and rain. Since the air has lower pressure, it rises through the atmosphere.

A tornado crosses farmland.

High-pressure air is usually cooler and drier than low-pressure air. It sinks through the atmosphere, pushing away air that is at a lower pressure. High-pressure air usually leads to clear skies and fine weather.

By studying the weather, meteorologists are able to predict weather patterns. Weather patterns can change daily or seasonally. Meteorologists alert us to severe storms that may be coming, such as blizzards, hurricanes, and tornadoes.

This book will take a look at some record-breaking storms and other extreme weather conditions. These events can be highly dangerous to people and other living things. It's good that you're only reading about these weather record breakers, and not experiencing them!

A thermometer measures temperature.

Hot and Dry

Do you like sunny days? Then check out St. Petersburg, Florida. The city had 768 sunny days in a row from 1967 to 1969! There may have been rain, but on each of those 768 days the Sun was out at some point.

Florida receives lots of sunshine every year.

How hot is too hot? The highest temperature ever recorded in the United States was 134°F in a place called Death Valley, California. On days like that, the temperature of the soil can reach 200°F. That's almost hot enough to boil water!

The Atacama Desert is one of the driest places on Earth.

Many scientists consider the Atacama Desert in Chile to be the driest place on Earth. Stable high-pressure systems form west of the Atacama, over the Pacific Ocean. They keep moisture-carrying storms away. Meanwhile, the Andes mountains to the east of the Atacama block moisture from flowing west. Temperatures in the Atacama Desert range from 32°F to 77°F, making the weather there dry, but not too hot.

The Big Chill

The colder air becomes, the less moisture it can carry. Because of this, very cold places like the North and South Poles get little snow.

Several species of penguins live in Antarctica.

Places such as the northeastern United States are frequently hit by blizzards. These storms are also called nor'easters. New York City has experienced some very notable nor'easters. In 1888, 21 inches of snow fell there over a couple of days. The 70-mile-per-hour wind gusts made by that nor'easter created 30-foot-high snowdrifts. About a century later, in 1996, 20 inches of snow fell during another New York City nor'easter. That time, the snowdrifts were "only" 20 feet high!

Record Breaker!
The world's coldest place is Vostok, Antarctica. In 1983, the temperature went down to −129°F!

−129°F

When blizzards make it unsafe to drive, some offices and schools close for the day.

When It Really Rains

There are ten different kinds of clouds. Steady, long-lasting rain comes mostly from nimbostratus clouds. These clouds hang low in the sky. They are usually thick and dark.

The top of Mount Wai'ale'ale in Kauai, Hawaii, seems to pull nimbostratus clouds toward itself. This mountain gets an average of 460 inches of rain each year. That's about 38 feet of precipitation! It rains more at Mount Wai'ale'ale than anywhere else in the United States.

On average, rain falls 350 days a year at Mount Wai'ale'ale in Kauai, Hawaii.

The rainiest place on Earth is the village of Cherrapunji, located in the state of Meghalaya, India. On average, 508 inches of rain fall there every year!

Every summer, monsoons blow warm, moist ocean air from the Indian Ocean over Cherrapunji. The air can't get over the Himalayas, an incredibly high mountain range near Cherrapunji, without first dropping its heavy rain.

Sometimes rain becomes hail. Hail can form when tiny raindrops get sucked upward high into a cloud. A hailstone that fell in Bangladesh in 1986 weighed more than 2 pounds!

When rain in a storm cloud freezes, it can form hailstones.

Eye of the Storm

Hurricanes are the world's most powerful and destructive storms. They begin over warm, tropical ocean water in summer and fall. As they move over land, they get weaker. Before they lose their strength, hurricanes can cause a lot of damage.

This photo, taken from space, clearly shows the eye of Hurricane Elena.

A hurricane can create a storm surge, or a rise in the sea level. Waves of ocean water sweep coastal areas during hurricanes. In 1900, a 15-foot-high storm surge drowned thousands of people in Galveston, Texas.

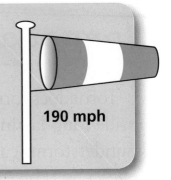
Hurricanes are called typhoons in the northwest Pacific Ocean and cyclones in the Indian Ocean. A 1970 cyclone in Bangladesh killed more than 300,000 people. It may have been the deadliest storm ever.

It is very still inside the eye, or center, of a hurricane. However, powerful winds surround it. Hurricane Andrew swept across southern Florida in 1992, generating winds of 164 miles per hour. Andrew caused 26 deaths and more than $26 billion in damage.

The wreckage of these homes was caused by Hurricane Andrew.

Tornadoes

Tornadoes form inside long-lasting, strong thunderstorms called supercells. The United States has about eight hundred tornadoes a year, more than anywhere else on Earth. With the exception of Alaska, every state in the country is vulnerable to tornadoes. Most tornadoes take place within the area of the Midwest known as Tornado Alley.

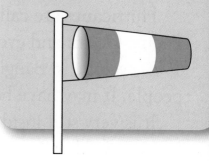

Record Breaker!

A record 148 tornadoes swept from Alabama to Ohio in just 24 hours in 1974!

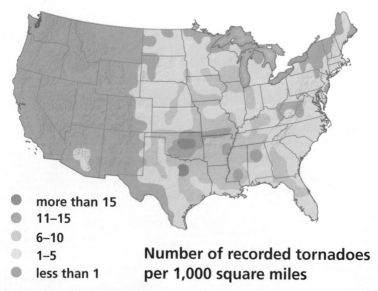

- more than 15
- 11–15
- 6–10
- 1–5
- less than 1

Number of recorded tornadoes per 1,000 square miles

Tornado winds can reach speeds of three hundred miles per hour! The fast-turning column of air in a tornado is called a vortex. A tornado's average diameter is 160 feet. The largest tornado ever measured hit northern Oklahoma in 1999. Its diameter was estimated at 5,250 feet, or almost one mile!

Tornadoes are famous for lifting cars, houses, and even trains. In 1949 in Oklahoma, a herd of cows was reportedly carried a quarter mile by a twister. Somehow many landed unharmed!

You can clearly see this tornado's spinning column of air.

Records

Some people live in places where the weather is mostly calm. Other people experience extreme weather situations like some of those listed here.

Hot and Dry

- Forty-eight percent of the continental United States was in drought during the summer of 2002.

- The driest place in the United States is Death Valley, California.

The Big Chill

- The coldest place in the United States, Prospect Creek, Alaska, recorded a temperature of –80°F.

- The most snow to fall in one day in the United States was 76 inches in Silver Lake, Colorado, in 1921.

When It Really Rains

• On August 24, 1906, a thunderstorm dropped nine inches of rain in just 40 minutes on Guinea, Virginia.

• In January 1909, at Helen Mine, California, 72 inches of rain fell during the month, a record for the continental United States.

Eye of the Storm

• On July 25, 1979, tropical storm Claudette showered the Houston suburb of Alvin with 43 inches of rain, a 24-hour record for the United States.

• 275 million trees were destroyed by a hurricane that hit New England on September 21, 1938.

Tornadoes

• On April 12, 1927, a tornado destroyed 235 of 247 buildings in the town of Rock Springs, Texas.

• On May 3–4, 1999, 59 tornadoes struck western and central Oklahoma.

Glossary

meteorologist   a scientist who studies Earth's atmosphere and weather

monsoons   strong, seasonal winds and rains that occur in Southeast Asia and India

nimbostratus cloud   a low, dark, and indistinctly outlined precipitation-bearing cloud

nor'easter   a type of blizzard that occurs on the northeastern coast of the United States

supercells   long-lasting, rotating thunderstorms that produce tornadoes

vortex   the turning column of air at the center of a tornado